31 Days of
Praying Psalm 91

Susan Chamberlain Shipe

Enjoy!
Susan

ISBN: 1986311325
ISBN-13: 978-1986311328
The 31 Day Series

All Scripture references from Bible Gateway
www.biblegateway.com

Published by:
The Vine Publications | Creston NC | U.S.A.

DEDICATION

For all the pray-ers.

CONTENTS

ACKNOWLEDGMENTS

Grateful appreciation to my family, my online tribe, and my personal cheerleaders - you know who you are! To the online sources that make book-writing easy and, (for me) fun: Bible Gateway, and CreateSpace.

Most of all to Jesus Christ, The Way, who gives me a heart overflowing with Hope!

Printables of Psalm 91 are
available on my blog:
www.hopehearthome.com
or by emailing me at
hopehearthome@gmail.com

1 PSALM 91

Psalm 91 NKJV

*He who dwells in the secret place of the Most High
Shall abide under the shadow of the Almighty.
I will say of the LORD, He is my refuge and my
fortress;
My God, in Him I will trust.
Surely He shall deliver you from the snare of the
fowler
And from the perilous pestilence.
He shall cover you with His feathers,
And under His wings you shall take refuge;
His truth shall be your shield and buckler.
You shall not be afraid of the terror by night,
Nor of the arrow that flies by day,
Nor of the pestilence that walks in darkness,
Nor of the destruction that lays waste at noonday.
A thousand may fall at your side,
And ten thousand at your right hand;*

But it shall not come near you.
Only with your eyes shall you look,
And see the reward of the wicked.
Because you have made the LORD, who is my refuge,
Even the Most High, your dwelling place,
No evil shall befall you,
Nor shall any plague come near your dwelling;
For He shall give His angels charge over you,
To keep you in all your ways.
In their hands they shall bear you up,
Lest you dash your foot against a stone.
You shall tread upon the lion and the cobra,
The young lion and the serpent you shall trample underfoot.
Because he has set his love upon Me, therefore I will deliver him;
I will set him on high, because he has known My name.
He shall call upon Me, and I will answer him;
I will be with him in trouble;
I will deliver him and honor him.
With long life I will satisfy him,
And show him My salvation.

Amen.
And, so we begin.

This beautiful Psalm of Moses is going to be our focus over the next 31 days. It would be awesome if each one of us memorized it like my dear friend Hettie did many years ago. Today she lives within the gates with the Most High God.

Before Hettie passed away we went to visit her. We sat in her parlor and there on the coffee table was her big family Bible opened to Psalm 91.

In her 90's Hettie's mind had given way to dementia and Alzheimer's but I took the chance. "Hettie, is Psalm 91 still your favorite? Can you recite it for us?"

Those sixteen verses, in beautiful King James, rolled off her southern Appalachian tongue like silk.

I looked at my husband, and Hettie's son and daughter-in-law and said, "The girl's still got it!"

Today, read aloud Psalm 91, slowly and intentionally. Begin to get familiar with its words.

2 PSALM 91 - PERSONALIZED

Psalm 91 NKJV

I dwell in the secret place of the Most High and I abide under the shadow of The Almighty. I say of the Lord, You are my Refuge and my Fortress; You are my God and You I trust. You will deliver me from the snare of the fowler and from the perilous pestilence. You will cover me with Your feathers and I will take refuge under Your wings. Your Truth will be my Shield and Buckler. I will not be afraid of the night terror or of the arrows that fly in the day, or of the pestilence that walks in darkness or of the destruction laying waste at noon. A thousand may fall at my side, and ten thousand at my right hand; but it will not come near me. Only my eyes will look and see the reward of the wicked ones. Because I have made the LORD, who is my Refuge, even the Most High God, my Dwelling Place, no evil will befall me nor will any plague/sickness come near my dwelling. For God will give His angels charge over me, to keep me in my way. The hands of the angels will hold me up, so I don't even stub a toe. I will tread on the lion and cobra, the young lion and serpent will I trample underfoot. Because I have set my love upon HIM, He will deliver me; He will lift me up because I know HIS NAME. I will call upon Him and He will answer me. God will be with me in trouble; He will deliver me and honor me. He will satisfy me with a long life and He will show me His Salvation.

Today, recite the psalm as a prayer over yourself. Get comfortable doing this.

3 PSALM 91 - TO PRAY OVER OTHERS

Psalm 91 NKJV

_____ dwells in the secret place of the Most High and
Shall abide under the shadow of the Almighty.

_____ will say of the Lord, He is my refuge and my
fortress;
My God, in Him I will trust.

Surely He shall deliver _____ from the snare of the
fowler
And from the perilous pestilence.
He shall cover _____ with His feathers,
And under His wings _____ shall take refuge;
His truth shall be _____ shield and buckler.

_____ shall not be afraid of the terror by night,

Nor of the arrow that flies by day,
Nor of the pestilence that walks in darkness,

Nor of the destruction that lays waste at noonday.

A thousand may fall at _____ side,
And ten thousand at _____right hand;
But it shall not come near _____.
Only with _____ eyes shall _____ look,
And see the reward of the wicked.

Because _____ has made the Lord, who is my refuge,
Even the Most High, _____ dwelling place,

No evil shall befall _____,
Nor shall any plague come near _____ dwelling;
For He shall give His angels charge over _____,
To keep _____ in all _____ ways.

In their hands they shall bear _____ up,
Lest _____ dash his or her foot against a stone.
_____ shall tread upon the lion and the cobra,
The young lion and the serpent _____ shall trample
underfoot.

Because _____ has set his or her love upon Me,
therefore I will deliver _____;
I will set _____ on high, because _____ has known My
name.

_____ shall call upon Me, and I will answer _____;
I will be with _____ in trouble;
I will deliver and honor _____.
With long life I will satisfy _____,
And show _____ My salvation.

Amen.

Today, pray Psalm 91 over a loved one. Put their name in the blanks.

4 DWELL

He who dwells in the secret place of the Most High shall abide under the shadow of the Almighty. Psalm 91.1

The year was 1988 - frustration was looming. My husband, then 10-year old son, and I were house hunting in the Boone NC area. We had vacationed in the region several times and now our goal was to move to the area. We wanted an old farmhouse and some acreage. We looked and looked. Finally our realtor suggested we look in the neighboring county where real estate prices were still affordable and within our budget. We happily took his suggestion!

As we followed behind our realtor driving the forty miles to Ashe County I said to my husband and son, "I'm tired of being on vacation. Tired of looking. I just want to live here."

Psalm 91, verse 1, in Susan-paraphrase, states: *She who lives permanently in - not visiting now and then - in that special secret place with God is legally bound to remain under the protection of Almighty God.*

The key to this protection? I must <u>dwell</u> in God's

Secret Place.

The Word is clear, God shares secrets with those who dwell with Him.

Indeed, the Sovereign Lord never does anything until he reveals his plans to his servants the prophets. Amos 3.7 (NLT)

Marriage is a good example - do we truly know our spouse until we have dwelt together for an extended time? I've been married to my husband for 34-years and I can just about guess what he is thinking or planning to do. Why? Because, we are co-residents of the same house, and we have developed intimacy.

As a committed believer, I have been dwelling with my heavenly Father for approximately 25-years and I can almost, with certainty, know how He will answer my prayers. Why? How? Because we abide together - my Father and me! I'm not going to ask Him for foolish things but I am going to be bold in asking things that I know line-up with His good, acceptable, and perfect will for my life or the life of my loved ones. I can be confident in those things because after 25-years of dwelling together, it is quite apparent I've gotten to know Him pretty well!

Moses wrote Psalm 91 - not David. In fact, those who document such things believe that Moses wrote the 90th and 91st Psalm within a space of time between Numbers chapter 15 and Deuteronomy chapter 34. I find that incredibly interesting.

If anyone knew about dwelling with God? It was Moses. I wonder did Moses write Psalm 91 as he stood on the mountain of Nebo, at the top of Pisgah, over Jericho ... as he looked out over the Promised Land of Milk and Honey; as God showed him what He had promised, after the moment God Himself said to him,

I will give it to your seed: I have allowed you to see it with your very own eyes but I will not let you go over there. Deuteronomy 34.4

Perhaps before he took his final breath he penned the following...

He who dwells in the secret place of the Most High SHALL abide under the shadow of the Almighty. I will say of the Lord, He is my Refuge and my Fortress; My God, in Him I will trust...He shall cover you with His feathers, and under His wings you shall take refuge; His truth shall be your Shield and Buckler.

Psalm 91.1,2,4

Today, I pray that I dwell with, remain in, my precious heavenly Father - I don't want to be an occasional visitor - one who has to knock on the door; I want to be a backdoor friend, welcomed at all hours of the day to hear Him say,

Because you have set your love on Me, I will deliver you; I will set you on high, because you have known My name. You will call upon Me and I will answer you. I will be with you in trouble; I will deliver you and honor you. With long life I will satisfy you and show you My salvation. Psalm 91.14-16 Selah

Today, consider the terms dwell and visit. Write down the pro's and con's of both. Then assess, are you a dweller or a visitor?

dwell.

31 Days of Praying Psalm 91

5 TRUST

I will say of the Lord, He is my refuge and my fortress; My God in Him I will trust. Psalm 91.2

Trust just may be the hardest thing to do.

Do I trust You, Lord?

In context Psalm 91.2 is making a declaration. The one who dwells in the secret place of the Most High God shall abide under the shadow of the Almighty... and, will say of the Lord:

HE IS MY REFUGE AND MY FORTRESS; MY GOD IN HIM I WILL TRUST.

We are making the assumption that Moses wrote Psalm 91. We know he wrote the 90th Psalm, as unidentified scripture goes - we can assume he wrote the following psalm also.

At the end of Moses' life these words would be most fitting. Let us reflect on Moses for a moment.

Raised in the palace of a Pharaoh - he had every luxury and advantage of any boy in Egypt. Everything changed for Moses when he found out he was an Israelite, who would have been a slave making bricks, if it hadn't been for his mother placing him in a waterproof basket and pushing him down the Nile River.

At the age of 40, he killed an Egyptian man. He fled to the desert, where he stayed forty years. And, at 80-years old he stood before the burning bush and heard the voice of God. (ref: Exodus 3)

The rest, they say, is history! True, bible history!

Moses led the enslaved Israelites out of Egypt after a 400-year captivity, promising them what God had told him - a land flowing with milk and honey and their freedom.

We know that the eleven-day journey ended up taking them 38-40 years. Whining, complaining, stubbornness, were the prohibiting factors to their arrival. It was so bad that God told them not one of the original people who fled Egypt's slavery would make it to the Promised Land - only their sons and daughters.

Even Moses, faithful Moses, was told that he would **see** the Promised Land, which flowed with milk and honey, with his eyes, but his foot would not **touch** its soil.

That is where we find the depth and meaning of the

words in Psalm 90 and 91.

As Moses stood on the Mount of Nebo, at the top of Pisgah, overlooking Jericho, he reflected on the last 40 or so years of his life. From a stuttering shepherd in Midian, to an old man at the end of his life, he knew, he felt the words...

Oh LORD, I have dwelt in Your secret place; I have made my abode under Your shadow. I can say, You are my Refuge and my Fortress, I trust in You.

Today, meditate on the word TRUST. Write down its meaning and search out scriptures with the word.

Susan Chamberlain Shipe

trust.

31 Days of Praying Psalm 91

6 DELIVER

Surely He shall deliver you from the snare of the fowler and from the perilous pestilence. Psalm 91.3

Snare of the fowler?

A fowler is a bird hunter, who would set out traps to catch the wee things. And, the reason? Temple sacrifices. And, the sacrifice had to make it to the altar alive...

And if the burnt sacrifice of his offering to the LORD is of birds, then he shall bring his offering turtledoves or young pigeons. Leviticus 1.14-17

"And he shall offer one of the turtledoves or young pigeons, such as he can afford..." Leviticus 14.30

Today, let's refer to the "trapper" as Satan.

Keep me from the snares they have laid for me, and from the traps of the workers of iniquity. Psalm 141.9

And a servant of the Lord must not quarrel but be gentle to all, able to teach, patient, in humility correcting those who are in opposition, if God perhaps will grant them repentance, so that they

*may know the truth, and that they (unbelievers)
may come to their senses and escape the snare of
the devil, having been taken captive by him to do his
will. 2 Timothy 2.24-26*

*Be sober, be vigilant; because your adversary the
devil walks about like a roaring lion, seeking whom
he may devour. 1 Peter 5.8*

*But deliver us from the evil one. (Jesus' words)
Matthew 6.13*

*I do not pray that You should take them out of the
world, but that You deliver them from the evil one.
(Jesus' words) John 17.15*

Perilous Pestilence?

Important to remember here that we are 99% sure
Moses wrote Psalm 91. He knew a thing or ten
about pestilence and plagues.

*Water becoming blood
Frogs
Lice
Flies
Sick cows and other livestock
Hail
Locusts*

Darkness
Death of the firstborn

Read Exodus chapters 7-11.

When we read Psalm 91.3 and as we pray the scriptures over ourselves, our homes, and our loved ones, perhaps verse 3 can be paraphrased like this:

Father God we ask You to deliver us from the traps Satan has set out for us - give us wisdom to discern his trappings, and, Lord, deliver us from physical sickness and spiritual attacks.

Today, if time allows, read the referenced chapters in Exodus and understand the power of Moses' prayer in Psalm 91.

deliver.

31 Days of Praying Psalm 91

7 REFUGE

He shall cover you with His feathers, and under His wings you shall take refuge. Psalm 91.4a-b

In 1945, a rumor circulated that the *National Geographic*[R] had published a story about a Yellowstone National Park ranger finding a burned mother hen under a tree after a ravaging forest fire. The story stated the ranger was saddened by the sight and with his boot gently pushed the burned body and three little chicks scurried out alive and well, untouched by the flames. The story is not true; however, just the picture of protection and safety that mother hen provided her chicks, is one of great heart-warming value.

Of even more value and encouragement is the image of God Himself covering us with His feathers and under His wings being a safe place of shelter.

In September of 2006 I was praying for my grandchildren's schools. Hannah was in the sixth grade and Simon in kindergarten - I prayed Psalm 91.4. As I prayed the Holy Spirit gave me a vision of an old-fashioned schoolhouse with God's protective, feathered wings hovering over the building. I sketched the vision so I could always remember the picture of His faithfulness.

Still to this day, I pray this prayer over their schools. Hannah is an undergrad student at Liberty University and Simon, after nine years of being homeschooled, is attending the local high school as a freshman.

The Mother Hen story might be false, but Psalm 91.4 is as real today as it was when Moses stood atop Mount Nebo, breathing his final breaths, and praying for his beloved brethren and their families as they were about to enter the promised land of milk and honey.

O Almighty God, the Most High God, You are my refuge and fortress. In You, O God I trust. Please insulate these precious people from the fires and tribulations they are about to face. Cover them with

Your holy, feathered wings of protection and give them safe passage and refuge. I pray.

Today, pray Psalm 91.4 over a loved one and let the images, written about today, permeate your mind and heart.

refuge.

31 Days of Praying Psalm 91

8 TRUTH

His truth shall be your shield and buckler. Psalm 91.4c

Truth.

Remember when Pilate asked Jesus, "What is truth?" (John 18.38)

If I had been there that day and knowing what I know today I would have looked at Pilate and said, "Sir, you are looking TRUTH right square in the eyes."

Jesus is our Truth. When Moses prayed these words he knew Yahweh to be his Truth.

The God-Truth who split the Red Sea.

The God-Truth who provided manna and quail.

The God-Truth who inscribed ten life commands into rock.

The God-Truth who...

Protected
Provided
Promoted
Prepared

and

Purposed him all his life.

Moses knew God's truth. He wore it as a shield and a buckler.

A buckler is armor for the arms! Moses was covered by truth and he trusted Him!

In Psalm 91 verse 4, the Hebrew word *chasah* is represented. *Chasah: to trust; to hope; to make someone a refuge.* In verse 4 it is illustrated as being nestled under God's wings for refuge.

Just like the vision I was given as I prayed Psalm 91 over the schools.

There IS refuge under God's wings. I cannot think of a safer place I'd rather be.

Today, write out your prayer of protection using

Psalm 91.4 as a guide.

truth.

31 Days of Praying Psalm 91

9 NO FEAR

You shall not be afraid of the terror by night, nor of the arrow that flies by day... Psalm 91.5

No fear.

I was always afraid of the dark. And, I still like night-lights!

In November 2003, when my husband broke his neck and was taken to the E.R. in Wheeling, W.Va in the middle of the night - he told the on-duty nurse, when she asked about calling his wife, "Wait until morning she does better with bad news when it's daylight!"

It seems bad news always comes at night. When that phone rings - it just sounds like bad news and I don't want to answer it.

Moses prayed, "O God I don't want my people to be afraid of night terror."

What about those arrows that fly by day?

Open assaults.

I believe for today, our trust in the Sovereign God must be so sharp and so real that nothing shakes us.

Nothing takes us by surprise.

The enemy of our soul doesn't care one whit if it's daytime or nighttime...he will attack whenever he darn well pleases.

Our TRUST Meter must be ramped up. Charged up. At the ready. Remember, when the terror comes at night or the arrow flies at day...

GAKAT. God Already Knows About This.

It may be the hardest thing we ever do but do it, we must. TRUST HIM.

Now, let's pray Psalm 91.5 in today's language.

Father God, my trust is in You and I don't want to be afraid. I want to lean on You and hide in You so heavily and deeply that nothing unravels me. Help me, O God to trust You more.

Today, actively participate in trusting God. Fill your tank. Adjust your meter. Plug in. Write out scriptures declaring your faith and trust in His sovereignty.

no fear.

31 Days of Praying Psalm 91

10 NO FEAR REPEAT

Nor of the pestilence that walks in darkness. Psalm 91.6a

More pestilence.

Still dark.

"The Lord will make the plague [pestilence] cling to you until He has consumed you from the land which you are going to possess." Deuteronomy 28.21

As we read Psalm 90 and 91, it is imperative we keep it in context. YES, we can pray Psalm 91 and personalize it for today but to 'understand' it we need to remember and realize the times in which it was written.

Moses (99% certain) wrote Psalm 91. He also wrote the first five books of the Old Testament. He knew a lot about plagues, pestilence, and the likes of such!

In Deuteronomy chapter 28, we learn the fourteen blessings of obedience and the fifty-three curses on disobedience. Yes, you read that right. Go look for yourself!

God was serious about obedience - He still is but now we are under the grace of our Savior, the Lord Jesus Christ. O! Thank You for the cross, Lord!

In Deuteronomy 28.21 we read the following:

But it shall come to pass, if you do not obey the voice of the LORD your God, to observe carefully all His commandments and His statutes which I (Moses) command you today, that all these curses will come upon you and overtake you...the Lord will make the plague [pestilence] cling to you until He has consumed you from the land which you are going to possess." Deuteronomy 28. v.15 and v.21

Whew.

So, IF Moses received those decrees from GOD HIMSELF, why wouldn't his final prayer include the protection, from the same, for his beloved people?

Today, read Deuteronomy 28. Take notes and ponder. Context. Remember scripture must be read IN CONTEXT!

no fear.

31 Days of Praying Psalm 91

11 NO FEAR REPEAT AGAIN

Nor of the destruction that lays waste at noonday. Psalm 91.6b

God's Word is rich.

O! How I love Your law! It is my meditation all the day. You, through Your commandments, make me wiser than my enemies; for they [commandments] are ever with me. Psalm 119.97

(Sidenote: Tradition tells us that King David wrote Psalm 119 to teach Solomon the alphabet! Not just the alphabet for writing but the spiritual alphabet!)

What does Psalm 91.6b say to us today? To fully understand 'the destruction that lays waste at noonday,' let's take a look at a reference to noonday in (again) Deuteronomy 28.

"The Lord will strike you with madness and blindness and confusion of heart. And you shall grope at noonday, as a blind man gropes in darkness; you shall not prosper in your ways; you shall be only oppressed and plundered continually, and no one shall save you." Deuteronomy 28.28-29

Whew (again).

Remember Deuteronomy 28, verses 15 through 68, speak to the curses for disobeying God. Moses knew a thing or two about disobedience. He led the

Israelites around that mountain for almost 40 years - when in all reality it should have taken them 11 days. He knew first-hand the stubborn disobedience of his people. He knew first-hand, his own stubborn refusal to believe GOD at that burning bush! (ref: Exodus 3)

Let's paraphrase Psalm 91.6 as we pray the Psalm:

Father God, I pray that sickness and illness will stay away from me and my house and, LORD, I pray that nothing blindsides us. That we recognize the ploys of the evil one as he tries to destroy us. Father God, open our eyes to Your Truth and keep us in Jesus' Name.

Today, continue contemplating Deuteronomy 28. And, revel in the grace of our Lord and Savior, Jesus Christ. O! Thank You for the cross, Lord.

no fear.

31 Days of Praying Psalm 91

12 VICTORY

A thousand may fall at your side...Psalm 91.7a

Today, just a few moments ago, my co-worker and I were praying, his family has suffered a myriad of 'bugs' this winter and as I prayed for him and his family I prayed...

Lord, in Jesus' Name I pray that the germs in L & L's home will fall dead - a thousand of them will fall and die.

Apparently Mr. L was downstairs in the kitchen because I could hear Mrs. L say, "AMEN TO THAT!"

When we pray Psalm 91 over ourselves and our loved ones there is no need to complicate it. It can be as simple as praying for 1,000 germs to die!

We are not to assume Moses is talking about victory in battle in Psalm 91.7 - he is still talking about the pestilence in verse 6!

Context...it's always about context!

Today, claim victory over something that is trying to lay claim to you by praying and believing God is able to eradicate 1,000 at your side!

victory.

31 Days of Praying Psalm 91

13 GREATER VICTORY

And ten thousand at your right hand...Psalm 91.7b

And Moses said to Joshua, "Choose us some men and go out, fight with Amalek. Tomorrow I will stand on the top of the hill with the rod of God in my hand." So Joshua did as Moses said to him, and fought with Amalek. And Moses, Aaron, and Hur went up to the top of the hill. And so it was, when Moses held up his hand, that Israel prevailed; and when he let down his hand, Amalek prevailed. But Moses' hands became heavy [weary of being held up]; so they took a stone and put it under him, and he sat on it. And Aaron and Hur supported his hands, one on one side, and the other on the other side; and his hands were steady until the going down of the sun. So Joshua defeated Amalek and his people with the edge of the sword. Exodus 17.9-13

Now, this was a battle. No question about it. People died and Joshua fought with a sword.

Moses was a smart man, he'd been around the block (or should we say mountain!) a time or two. He knew God - he also knew there was an enemy.

As he prayed on Mount Nebo at the end of his life it is safe to believe his prayer went something like this:

Lord, You have been my dwelling place - before the

mountains were formed, before the earth was - YOU WERE. These people that you gave me, LORD, they are about to go into that land of promise - that land filled with good things and I pray that You O LORD will scatter the enemies and destroy all manner of plague and pestilence - cause them to fall at their right hand. Go before them O LORD and make their way safe and sure. Amen

Today, the enemy seeking to destroy us is Satan himself. Pray these Psalm 91 prayers and believe for VICTORY.

Susan Chamberlain Shipe

victory.

31 Days of Praying Psalm 91

14 PROTECTION

But it shall not come near you...Psalm 91.7c

A hedge of protection.

So Satan answered the LORD and said, "Does Job fear God for nothing? Have You not made a hedge around him, around his household, and around all that he has on every side? You have blessed the work of his hands, and his possessions have increased in the land..." Job 1.9-10

Do you pray those words?

I do. All the time.

Father God, in Jesus' Name, I ask You to put a hedge of protection around my family - that no harm come upon them.

He will not allow your foot to be moved; He who keeps you will not slumber. Behold, He who keeps Israel shall neither slumber nor sleep. Psalm 121.3-4

"No man shall be able to stand before you all the days of your life; as I was with Moses, so I will be with you. I will not leave you nor forsake you..." Joshua 1.5

Fear not, I am with you; be not dismayed, for I am your God. I will strengthen you, yes, I will help you, I will uphold you with My righteous right hand. Isaiah 41.10

A hedge of protection.

God loves us to pray His Word back to Him. Keep these scriptures in your journal, in your purse, just keep them near and pray them over your loved ones. Moses did - he stood on Mount Nebo and held his arms out and declared...

Jehovah LORD, may a thousand plagues fall at their side and 10,000 enemies at their right hand --- but let it NOT come near them. Selah.

Today, realize you are in a battle with the enemy of your soul and with The Word, claim victory!

Susan Chamberlain Shipe

protection.

31 Days of Praying Psalm 91

15 SIGHT

Only with your eyes shall you look, and see the reward of the wicked. Psalm 91.8

Moses is now saying to his people, although they cannot hear nor see him, "Just open your eyes and see how the LORD is protecting you and taking care of those who are evil and wicked. "

We must never forget the righteousness of our righteous God. There **will be** reward for the wicked and it won't be pretty.

Because we live on "this" side of The Cross, believers in Jesus Christ are covered by His grace - we will **never** be subject to God's wrath. **NEVER.** We have been "saved" from the Wrath of God. (ref: Romans 5.9)

Moses didn't have the advantage of Calvary, as we do, but by faith he believed.

The Israelites, whom Moses led in the desert for nearly 40 years, were rascals - but he loved them dearly and prayed earnestly for them. How much more can **we** pray his words in Psalm 91 over ourselves, our loved ones, and our homes? Moses gave us a pattern for prayer and it is one we can be bold in repeating.

Today, read aloud (again) Psalm 91. Hopefully, the words are beginning to have true understanding. Perhaps write the Psalm out.

sight.

31 Days of Praying Psalm 91

16 CHOOSE

Because you have made the LORD, who is my refuge.... Psalm 91.9a

LORD, because these people have made You, my refuge, their own refuge.....no evil shall befall them...no sickness will come near their dwelling...

THIS is exactly what Moses is believing and praying.

It all comes down to choice, doesn't it? Are we going to receive and obey? Or, are we going to ignore and disobey?

Yes, we are under grace - but let us never cheapen the grace of our Almighty God. God's gift of grace should spur us on to good works not be a license for doing wrong.

Do we see the difference?

Every single day we are faced with decisions and choices - God is not standing over us waving a magic wand - we have to choose.

Choose you THIS DAY whom you will serve? From Joshua 24.14-16

Moses was a man full of the goodness of the LORD and faith. History tells us the Israelites didn't cross over into the Promised Land and everything turned out sunshine and rainbows. It didn't and the reason? BAD CHOICES. WRONG DECISIONS.

Choose today. Every day we have a choice.

Today, think back on some decisions and choices you've had to make in your life. If able, would you go back and change? Don't get into the regret trap but start thinking on how to go forward.

choose.

31 Days of Praying Psalm 91

17 MORE CHOOSING

Even the Most High your dwelling place.... Psalm 91.9b

Moses you know how to hit repeat, don't you?

Most of us have put a song on repeat, right? Your favorite CD and you hit track 4 repeat! There have been seasons in my life when a SELAH CD was on repeat wherever I went. The song? *You Are My Hiding Place.* (ref: Psalm 32.7)

Our friend Moses is on repeat...

Because you have made the LORD, who is my refuge, even the Most High, your dwelling place, no evil shall befall you, nor shall any plague come near your dwelling...

On Day 4 we talked about the difference between visiting and dwelling. There is a choice to be made, isn't there?

Do I want to dwell in the Secret Place? Or, am I more comfortable visiting now and then?

The blessing comes in the dwelling.

The staying.

Father God, I have made You my Refuge, I dwell in the Secret Place of the Most High God. Therefore, no evil shall befall me, nor shall any disease come near our dwelling. Amen in Jesus' Name.

Today, can you pray this prayer? What is holding you back? What is hindering you?

choose.

31 Days of Praying Psalm 91

18 CONSEQUENCES

No evil shall befall you.... Psalm 91.10a

I do not like writing about or thinking about the evil one but today we are going to.

Everything changed the day in The Garden when Eve, and Adam with her, listened to the Serpent and took a bite out of the forbidden fruit. He has been an active menace ever since.

Here are some things, we as Jesus-followers, must guard against:

Beware brethren, lest there be in any of you an evil heart of unbelief in departing from the living God. Hebrews 3.12

My brethren, do not hold the faith of our Lord Jesus Christ, the Lord of glory with partiality...have you not shown partiality among yourselves, and become judges with evil thoughts? James 2.1,4

But now you boast in your arrogance. All such boasting is evil. James 4.16

Let love be without hypocrisy. Abhor what is evil. Cling to what is good. Romans 12.9

Whoever transgresses and does not abide in the doctrine of Christ does not have God. He who abides in the doctrine of Christ has both the Father and Son. If anyone comes to you and does not bring this doctrine, do not receive him into your house nor greet him; for he who greets him shares in his evil deeds. 2 John verses 9-11

Immorality must be judged: 1 Corinthians 5.9-13

Abstain [run and flee] from every form of evil. 1 Thessalonians 5.22

Above all, taking the shield of faith with which you will be able to quench all the fiery darts of the wicked [evil] one. Ephesians 6.16

There is no doubt Moses knew about evil - of course he did, but today our struggle looks differently and these scriptures need to be read in context, (which means read before and after the referenced verses!) and studied.

We must never be found ignorant of the ploys of the devil. He will try every trick in his arsenal to get to us.

O God, that his evil does not befall us.

Today, read Ephesians 6.10-18. Write it out.

consequence.

31 Days of Praying Psalm 91

19 IMMUNITY

**Nor shall any plague come near your dwelling....
Psalm 91.10b**

Influenza Type A

Influenza Type B

Influenza Type C

E.Coli

E.Boli

When we read Psalm 91 and read words like pestilence and plague, we kind of think *we're immune to stuff like that today.*

Are we?

Do you remember the Bird Flu? All the hype in the news and people walking through airports with face masks on? You want to know what I did? I printed out Psalm 91 and taped it to our door with this warning: NOT TODAY SATAN!

I have so much faith in God's Word - I believe every dotted i and crossed t and I think its relevance is for TODAY.

I think it's high time we fight the enemy of our souls and bodies with GOD'S WORD. That is why I think studying Psalm 91, praying it, believing it, and standing on it is imperative for believers in the 21st Century.

I believe there is POWER in its words.

Today, are you daring enough to print out the words of Psalm 91 and tape them to the door? NOT TODAY SATAN, NOT TOMORROW EITHER.

immunity.

31 Days of Praying Psalm 91

20 ANGELS

**For He shall give His angels charge over you...
Psalm 91.11a**

Let's talk about angels, shall we?

People do not become angels when they die.

God never "needs" another angel.

People cannot be angels.

Angels can manifest as people (ref: Genesis 18).

Let me explain... I do believe God can do any, and I mean anything, and I also believe there are "angels unaware." I've actually had real life encounters with them.

But when I read on Facebook that "God needed another angel so He took so and so," I cringe --- it just isn't true.

God created angels. They are created beings. Nowhere in scripture are they referred to as feminine - they are male in angel-gender! For example: Michael, Gabriel, *Antonio, Caleb...oh wait.*

Hannah used to spend her summers with us in North Carolina. I worked outside the home and every morning when we left the house, we would stop out front and pray and ask God to release His guard angels over the house and property. Antonio stood on the north side of the house and Caleb took the south side. We were so serious about our prayer that I believe 'in the spirit' we saw them! It was a faith-building exercise.

Remember, ONLY God can release His angels. **We** cannot order them - we must pray and ask our heavenly Father to give them charge.

I have many angel stories - perhaps one day I will share them in a book!

Today, think about and write down the people, places, and things you would like God to charge His angels with.

angels.

31 Days of Praying Psalm 91

21 KEPT

To keep you in all your ways. Psalm 91.11b

Let's continue talking about angels, shall we?

Take heed that you do not despise one of these little ones, for I say to you that in heaven their angels always see the face of My Father who is in heaven. Matthew 18.10 (Jesus speaking.)

Simon used to stand in his crib and look up into the corner of his room. Like, **all the time.** He would play with his cars and action figures while sitting on the floor talking to them and suddenly he would look up into that corner and then do something unrelated to the toys he was playing with! It was strange. One day my daughter and I were talking about it and she asked if that was normal behavior! I told her what I sincerely believed - he had an angel watching over him and it hung out up in the corner of his room. Or, probably he was so tall, Simon looked at his face not his body!

Do I really believe that? Oh, yes I do!

[Dr. Billy Graham, observing the plural in this text, concluded that each **believer** must have at least two angels whose assigned duty it is to protect them.

Psalm 91.4 speaks of God "covering us with His feathers" and mentions that we are under His "wings." Since God has no feathers or wings, some have suggested that these feathers and wings speak of our guardian angels' wings, which protectively cover us to keep us from falling, getting lost, or stumbling into unknown dangers in the unseen realm of the spirit. (reference: Acts 8.26; Exodus 3.2 and 4) Note by Marilyn Hickey, Spirit-Filled Life Bible.]

We aren't finished discussing angels!

Today, reflect on some times in your own life when perhaps there was angelic activity around you.

kept.

31 Days of Praying Psalm 91

22 HELD

In their hands they shall bear [lift] you up. Psalm 91.12a

In their hands...held.

There Moses stood atop Mount Nebo. He knew he had come to the end of his life. He wasn't sick, and he really wasn't old, but God had told him he would not go into the Promised Land with the others.

Moses was one hundred and twenty years old when he died. His eyes were not dim nor his natural vigor diminished. Deuteronomy 34.7

In their [the angels'] hands they shall bear you up.

Let's jump into the New Testament for a minute and see this scripture quoted...by none other than Satan himself.

Jesus had just been baptized by John the Baptizer. Now, The Spirit (HOLY SPIRIT) led Him into the wilderness to be tempted by the devil. Forty days of fasting was complete and Jesus was hungry. At that precise time, the stinking tempter shows up.

If you are the Son of God, command these stones become bread for you, Satan said.

Jesus said back to him, Man shall not live by bread alone but by every word that proceeds from My Father's mouth.

Satan continued, If You are the Son of God, throw Yourself down. It says "He [God] will give His angels charge over You and in their hands they will bear you up ..."

The tempter and Jesus went back and forth for several rounds.

Then the devil left Him, and behold, angels came and ministered to Him. Matthew 4.11

Today, read Matthew 4.1-11 and Hebrews 1.14. Write your observations down.

held.

31 Days of Praying Psalm 91

23 SAFETY

Lest you dash your foot against a stone. Psalm 91.12b

Not even the stubbing of a toe!

Seriously?

That's what it says.

I know there are worse things than a stubbed toe, but man, it hurts. I've done it more than a few times - now, when I get up in the middle of the night I use my hands to guide me away from the dreaded iron leg of the side table I have to pass on my way to the rest room!

On a cold November night in 2003 in Wheeling, West Virginia, my husband fell out of an 18-wheeler and laid on the asphalt parking lot for (perhaps) hours. At the very same time he fell, my son in South Florida was woken from a dream, in his spirit he heard, "Get out of bed and on the floor and pray for your stepdad - he's had an accident." My son did exactly what he was told - he laid on that hard wooden floor until he felt a release in prayer.

The next morning I got the phone call from the emergency room nurse that my husband had broken his neck. I began making the phone calls to my kids to tell them I would be making a trip to Wheeling. When I told the son who had been praying through the night - I could tell by his voice that he was shocked. He told me about his experience and the dream. We deduced he prayed the same exact hours my husband laid in the parking lot.

You might ask what my son prayed that fateful night? He prayed the only prayer he knew to pray as he didn't know what was going on. "God, in Jesus' Name I pray you surround Lowell with Your many angels and help him."

After the shock of the phone call, Mark asked me what kind of accident he had. When I told him that Lowell had fallen out of his parked rig - he let out an #$%&! "Oh wow," he said, "I saw in my dream that it wasn't a typical accident - there were no moving vehicles - just an injury."

For He shall give His angels charge over you, to keep you in all your ways, in their hands they shall bear you up, lest you dash your foot against a stone. Psalm 91.11-12

Yes, my husband broke his neck that night and he

wore a halo brace for six and one-half months - but he had no paralysis.

The angels held him and provided safety from severe injury and death.

Today, please consider the still small voice you sometimes hear - consider your response. It is imperative we pray when the Spirit speaks.

safety.

31 Days of Praying Psalm 91

24 COURAGE

You shall tread upon the lion and cobra... Psalm 91.13a

tread: to walk, go, tread, trample, march. This word, occurring more than sixty times in the Old Testament, suggests a more forceful activity than mere walking. "Marching" or "treading" would best render this Hebrew word **darach.** From this verb comes the noun **derech**, meaning "road," "path," or "way," whether an actual street or the path one habitually treads in life. (Word Wealth; Spirit-Filled Life Bible.)

*Every place on which the sole of your foot treads shall be yours: from the wilderness and Lebanon, from the river, the River Euphrates, even to the Western [Mediterranean] Sea, shall be your territory. No man shall be able to stand against [before] you; the LORD your God will put the dread of you and the fear of you upon all the land where you **tread,** just as He has said to you. Deuteronomy 11.24-25*

These were words spoken by Moses to the Israelites, the <u>adult</u> Israelites. Moses is clear to point out, *Know today that I do not speak with your children, who have not known...(Deuteronomy 11.2)*

Moses was reminding the adults to "carefully keep all these commandments."

Now, we look back and know they did NOT keep all the commandments. Now, we see Moses on Mount Nebo, at the end of his life and he is fervently praying over the children of those rebellious adult Israelites.

You will march upon the lion and cobra...as you march into The Promised Land.

Today's application? *And He [Jesus] said to them...Behold I give you the authority to trample on serpents and scorpions, and over all the power of the enemy, and nothing shall by any means hurt you. (Luke 10.19)* Have courage.

courage.

31 Days of Praying Psalm 91

25 BRAVE

The young lion and the serpent you shall trample underfoot. Psalm 91.13b

But since then there has not arisen in Israel a prophet like Moses, whom the LORD knew face-to-face, in all the signs and wonders which the LORD sent him to do in the land of Egypt, before Pharaoh, before all his servants, and in all his land, and by all that mighty power and all the great terror which Moses performed in the sight of all Israel. Deuteronomy 34.10-12

What an epitaph.

I believe as Moses stood on Mount Nebo, looking down on the Israelites as they were to cross over the Jordan River, led by Moses' successor Joshua, into the Promised Land, the land flowing with milk and honey - Moses prophesied.

A victory.

You shall tread upon the lion and the cobra, the young lion and the serpent you shall trample underfoot.

It is possible Moses prophesied over the people - the things that they were most afraid of they would conquer. He spoke courage and bravery over them.

Jesus did the same thing in Luke 10.19; Paul in Romans 16.20.

And the God of peace will crush Satan under your feet shortly...Romans 16.20

Today we face lions and serpents on a daily basis! They may not be four-legged, or slither on the ground, but we are being attacked every single day by the enemy of our soul. How will you apply Moses' words to your everyday battles?

brave.

31 Days of Praying Psalm 91

26 LOVE

Because he has set his love upon Me, therefore I will deliver him; Psalm 91.14a

Now, the LORD speaks through Moses about His own chosen one.

For example:

Because Susan has set her love upon Me, therefore I will deliver Susan.

Pretty powerful, eh? After we finish all sixteen verses of Psalm 91, I promise you will have a whole new outlook on praying this portion of scripture over yourself, your loved ones and your home!

These last three verses of the chapter is God speaking through Moses' lips. Is that not incredible?

Today begin writing this verse with your name and then the name of a loved one.

Susan Chamberlain Shipe

love.

31 Days of Praying Psalm 91

27 POSITION

I will set him on high, because he has known My Name; Psalm 91.14b

[The Lord continues to speak through Moses about His chosen one.]

I would like to imagine Moses atop of Mount Nebo praying like this:

Because Joshua has set his love on You, Adonai, therefore You will deliver him; You will set Joshua on high, because Joshua has known Your Name.

Moses' successor was Joshua. He was Moses' assistant as seen in Exodus 24.13. Joshua was now in the position of leader and he would be the one to take the Israelites across the Jordan and into the Promised Land.

Not because Joshua was special or better than any other man but because he loved God. He knew His name. God honors those who honor Him.

We see Joshua in Numbers 13, along with Caleb and eleven other men, as Moses sends them to "spy" on the land of Canaanites. These were the people who lived along the banks of the Jordan.

Joshua and Caleb were true leaders and when they returned to Moses, forty days after their spy assignment, they brought back a good report. But the other eleven men brought negative reports and put fear into the Israelites. Joshua and Caleb were ready, *Let us go up at once and take possession, for we are well able to overcome it. Numbers 13.30*

Position. God honors those who honor Him.

Today, read Numbers 13 in its entirety. Write out your meditation.

position.

31 Days of Praying Psalm 91

28 ANSWER

**He shall call upon Me, and I will answer him...
Psalm 91.15a**

[The Lord continues to speak through Moses about His chosen one.]

I want to focus on Caleb today. Remember, Caleb was one of the men sent to spy out the land of the Canaanites (Numbers 13).

We learn in Numbers 14 that the Israelites chose to believe the eleven spies who gave a bad spy report. The scene must have been ugly.

And all the children of Israel complained against Moses and Aaron, and the whole congregation said to them, "If only we had died in the land of Egypt! Or, if only we had died in this wilderness! Why has the LORD brought us to this land to fall by the sword, that our wives and children should become victims? Would it not be better for us to return to Egypt?" Numbers 14.2-3

WHAT?

I can't even.

Or, can I?

Hold on because we are going on the scripture train! Ready? All aboard!

God was not pleased with the outcry and whining of the Israelites. I mean, He was ready to strike every last one of them down. Moses stepped in and pled their case - pleaded and begged God to show mercy and not His might. Moses reminded God...

The Lord is longsuffering and abundant in mercy, forgiving iniquity and transgressions...(Numbers 14.18)

Then the LORD said, "I have pardoned, according to your word..." (Numbers 14.20)

And, then God Himself calls out Caleb...

But My servant Caleb, because he has a different spirit in him and has followed Me fully, I will bring into the land where he went, and his descendants shall inherit it. (Numbers 14.24)

Remember, this is all about "calling upon God and being answered by Him." Now, we jump way over to Joshua 14.

[Note: Psalm 91 was written at the close of Deuteronomy 34, written by Moses at the end of his life.]

Caleb Inherits Hebron Joshua 14.6-15

Caleb is now 85-years old. He and some others went to Joshua in Gilgal. Caleb said to Joshua, *You know the word which the LORD said to Moses the man of*

God concerning you and me in Kadesh Barnea. I was forty-years old when Moses the servant of the LORD sent me from Kadesh Barnea to spy out the land, and I brought back word to him as it was in my heart...so Moses swore on that day saying, 'Surely the land where your foot has trodden shall be your inheritance and your children's forever, because you have WHOLLY FOLLOWED THE LORD MY GOD.' (Joshua 14.6-9)

Caleb went on talking and reminding Joshua of all the things Moses had said to him regarding the inheritance of the land for himself and his children. Caleb also told Joshua he was healthy and strong for his 85-years and was able to fight and go to war to protect the land.

Caleb continued calling upon Moses' promise, through Joshua, and trusting God to answer him.

And Joshua blessed him, and gave Hebron to Caleb the son of Jephunneh as an inheritance. (Joshua 14.13)

...he shall call upon Me and I will answer him.

Today, what are YOU asking God for? Read all the referenced scriptures in today's devotion and then answer this question, "Does my life honor God the way Caleb's did?"

answer.

31 Days of Praying Psalm 91

29 TROUBLE

I will be with him in trouble... Psalm 91.15b

[The Lord continues to speak through Moses about His chosen one.]

Have you ever been in a lot of trouble? The kind you weren't sure you'd be able to get out of?

I could have been, but the mercy of the Lord protected me.

I deserved the trouble for my foolish actions. I knew better. I was impulsive and stupid (truly).

It was during my running-away-from-God years. I knew the Lord, but if truth be told I didn't like Him very much at that time. I did the dumb deed and I couldn't take it back.

But the God of prodigals was with me in my trouble.

Today, has God ever protected you in or from

trouble?

trouble.

31 Days of Praying Psalm 91

30 HONOR

I will deliver him and honor him... Psalm 91.15c

[The Lord continues to speak through Moses about His chosen one.]

I could have been. I should have been. In some mighty big trouble but it never materialized.

By the kind mercy of God, I was delivered.

A lot of things have happened to me since that time and the very best thing was my rededication to the Lord in 1992.

I will never forget the night. I knelt all alone at an altar and told the Lord from then on I was "all in." I wasn't going to be one of those Christians with one foot in the world and one foot in the kingdom. I was finished with foolish things and moving on to God things.

I've never looked back. I've never regretted my decision that night in 1992.

The Lord, in His mercy and by His grace, delivered me and honors me every day of my life.

I prefer Him over anyone or anything else.

He is my Beloved and I am His daughter.

Moses, thank you for praying this prayer, I have

made it my own.

Today, think back on the time of your deliverance. Aren't you grateful? Write a letter of gratitude to your Heavenly Father. He will honor you as you honor Him.

honor.

31 Days of Praying Psalm 91

31 SALVATION

With long life I will satisfy him, and show him My salvation. Psalm 91.16

[The Lord continues to speak through Moses about His chosen one.]

Once again, let's step on top of Mount Nebo with our brother and friend Moses. He looks down and can see the great River Jordan, a sea of people - "his" people, the children of Israel. The sons and daughters of the Israelites he rescued from Egypt. There they stood on the banks of the great river, ready to cross over into the land they were promised forty years before.

They were being led by Joshua, Moses' faithful assistant, now their leader.

Moses had just written his last two memoirs, Psalm 90 and 91. I would imagine he was sad. He was still in good health yet the LORD Himself had told him he would not go into The Promised Land with the others.

With a grand sweeping of his hand, perhaps in a final blessing, he declares:

O LORD, satisfy them with long life and show them Your Salvation.

Today, read Psalm 90 and 91 as one continuous psalm. Are you a recipient of His salvation?

salvation.

31 Days of Praying Psalm 91

TEHILLIM (PSALMS) 90 AND 91

From The Complete Jewish Bible
(translation by David H. Stern)

A Prayer of Moshe, the man of God:

Adonai, you have been our dwelling place in every generation. Before the mountains were born, before you had formed the earth and the world, from eternity past to eternity future, you are God.

You bring frail mortals to the point of being crushed, then say, "People, repent!" For from your viewpoint a thousand years are merely like yesterday or a night watch. When you sweep them away, they become like sleep; by morning they are like growing grass, growing and flowering in the morning, but by evening cut down and dried up.

For we are destroyed by your anger, overwhelmed by your wrath. You have placed our faults before you, our secret sins in the full light of your presence.

All our days ebb away under your wrath; our years die away like a sigh. The span of our life is seventy years, or if we are strong, eighty; yet at best it is toil and sorrow, over in a moment, and then we are gone.

Who grasps the power of your anger and wrath to the degree that the fear due you should inspire? So teach us to count our days, so that we will become wise.

Return, ADONAI! How long must it go on? Take pity on your servants! Fill us at daybreak with your love, so that we can sing for joy as long as we live. Let our joy last as long as the time you made us suffer, for as many years as we experienced trouble.

Show your deeds to your servants and your glory to their children. May the favor of Adonai our God be on us, prosper for us all the work that we do - yes, prosper the work that we do.

You who live in the shelter of 'Elyon, who spend your nights in the shadow of Shaddai, who say to ADONAI, "My refuge! My fortress! My God, in whom I trust!" - he will rescue you from the trap of the hunter and from the plague of calamities; he will cover you with his pinions, and under his wings you will find refuge; his truth is a shield and protection.

You will not fear the terrors of night or the arrow

that flies by day, or the plague that roams in the dark, or the scourge that wreaks havoc at noon. A thousand may fall at your side, ten thousand at your right hand; but it won't come near you. Only keep your eyes open, and you will see how the wicked are punished.

For you have made ADONAI, the Most High, who is my refuge, your dwelling-place. No disaster will happen to you, no calamity will come near your tent; for he will order his angels to care for you and guard you wherever you go. They will carry you in their hands, so that you won't trip on a stone. You will tread down lions and snakes, young lions and serpents you will trample underfoot.

"Because he loves me, I will rescue him; because he knows my name, I will protect him. He will call on me, and I will answer him. I will be with him when he is in trouble. I will extricate him and bring him honor. I will satisfy him with long life and show him my salvation."

Other Books by Susan:

- A Pruned Branch - a 365-day devotion/journal
- 31 Days of Hope
- 31 Days of Christmas
- 31 Days in Proverbs
- 31 Days in the Gospel of John
- 40 Days of Lent
- 31 Days of Haiku on Black and White
- The Best of HopeHeartHome Condensed Volume
- 31 Days Inside Matthew 6
- 31 Days of Praying Psalm 91
- Five Minute Friday
- How To Work @ Home Productively & Successfully
- Malchus, a read-aloud Easter story (ebook only)
- The Miracle of the Manger (ebook only)

Susan can be found musing several times a week at
www.hopehearthome.com
Visit Susan's author page at Amazon:
Susan Shipe
www.amazon.com/-/e/B00APZO7N6

If you enjoyed this book or received value from it in any way, then I'd like to ask you for a favor: would you be kind enough to leave a review for this book on Amazon? It would be greatly appreciated!

ABOUT THE AUTHOR

 A writer since the age of eight when she and her neighborhood friend wrote, edited, published, and distributed The Manor News. Things have changed since publishing with the five and dime stamp lettering set!

The Lord delivered a message of Hope deep within Susan's soul in 2002. Jesus, the Hope-giver met her in her hour of need and her heart overflowed with Hope.

Susan is Mom to three adult children, Mimzy to two fantastic grands, and Other Mom to several others! Today, she enjoys blogging, writing short devotions and short stories from her home in the Appalachian Mountain Range of the Blue Ridge Mountains in northwestern North Carolina, which she shares with her husband of thirty-plus years, Lowell, and their beloved dog, Sam.

Susan can be found musing several times a week at hopehearthome.com

Her life purpose: That I may walk worthy of the

Lord, fully pleasing Him, being fruitful in every good work and increasing in the knowledge of God. Colossians 1.10

Her life vision: I have no greater joy than to hear that my children walk in Truth. 3 John 4

Made in the USA
Columbia, SC
28 December 2021